P9-BYD-043

WITHDRAWN

PIC

Eider

Canvasback

Wood Duck

Blue-winged

out of print
out of print
not rare

Mickey's Class Play

By Judith Caseley

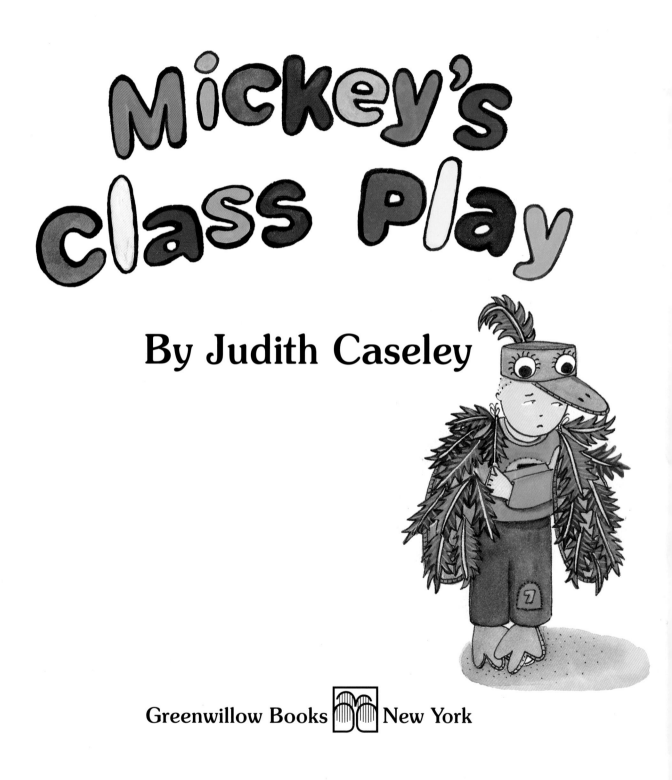

Greenwillow Books ⌘ New York

NEWTON FREE LIBRARY
NEWTON, MASS.

J
Fic

With special thanks to Deirdre Humphrey

Watercolor paints, colored
pencils, and a black pen were
used for the full-color art.
The text type is Souvenir Medium BT.
Copyright © 1998 by Judith Caseley
All rights reserved. No part
of this book may be reproduced
or utilized in any form or by any
means, electronic or mechanical,
including photocopying, recording,
or by any information storage
and retrieval system, without
permission in writing from the
Publisher, Greenwillow Books,
a division of William Morrow &
Company, Inc., 1350 Avenue of
the Americas, New York, NY 10019.
www.williammorrow.com
Printed in Hong Kong by South
China Printing Company (1988) Ltd.
First Edition
10 9 8 7 6 5 4 3 2 1

LIBRARY OF CONGRESS
CATALOGING-IN-PUBLICATION DATA
Caseley, Judith
Mickey's class play / by Judith
Caseley.
       p.   cm.
Summary: With the help of his family,
Mickey enjoys being
a duck in the class play.
ISBN 0-688-15405-0 (trade).
ISBN 0-688-15406-9 (lib. bdg.)
[1. Plays—Fiction.   2. Schools—
Fiction.   3. Family life—Fiction.]
I. Title.   PZ7.C2677Mi   1998
[E]—dc21   97-33036   CIP   AC

For

teachers

everywhere

When Mickey announced that his class was putting
on a play, Papa said, "How wonderful!"
Mama said, "Do I have to make you a costume?"
Jenna said, "I'll help you rehearse your lines."

The play was called *A Celebration of Animals*.
Mickey's teacher, Mrs. Humphrey, gave every child
in the class an animal part and a script.
She made three children kangaroos and two children
ladybugs and four children ducks and two children spiders
and three children cats and two children butterflies.

On the front page of Mickey's script, in big red letters, was the word *DUCK*, and a picture of one.

"I don't want to be a duck," said Mickey. "I don't like to quack."

"I don't want to be a spider," said Alexis. "Spiders are scary."

"Can we switch?" Mickey asked his teacher.

Mrs. Humphrey said yes, but then Amanda wanted to
be a cat and William said that ladybugs were for girls
and Ian said that he liked dogs much better than cats.
"Everybody has to keep his or her own part," said
Mrs. Humphrey.

Mickey was a grouchy duck until Jenna read
him the play.
"You get to sing a song and hop and flap
your wings," said Jenna. "And you even
get to hatch."
"I'm glad I'm a duck," said Mickey.

The art teacher helped the children make
their costumes.
The ducks made yellow beaks out of paper
and feathery white wings,
and the cats cut out little black ears,
and the butterflies painted fancy wings,
and the ladybugs colored big black spots,
and the kangaroos glued pouches out of felt,
and the spiders drew webs on their beanies.

The class rehearsed almost every day.

The kangaroos were happy because they got to jump around a lot.

The ducks were happy because they were the only ones with feathers.

The ladybugs were happy
because they had black spots.
(Mrs. Humphrey wouldn't
let them fly.)

The cats were happy
because they meowed
like crazy.
(They liked their whiskers
and long tails, too.)

The spiders were happy because they had more legs than anybody else. (Alexis said that she was a pretty spider.)

The butterflies were happy because they were all different colors, and their antennae shook when they jumped.

They all felt special in their own ways, which made
Mrs. Humphrey happy because she said that the
play was about celebrating your differences.
She told the children to practice at home every
single day.

Sometimes Mickey rehearsed with Jenna after school.

Sometimes he rehearsed with Papa while they were digging in the garden.

Once Mickey forgot, and he woke up at midnight and wanted to practice. Mama made him wait until breakfast time.

The day the play was to be presented, Mrs.
Humphrey gave the children their costumes.
"I'll see you all this evening," she told them.
"Six o'clock sharp, dressed and ready."

Mickey went home and practiced just one last
time, in the backyard with Jenna. He put his
costume on the picnic bench and made believe
that the table was the stage. Jenna clapped loudly
until Mama called them in for supper.

Mickey was so excited he could barely eat.
He cleared his plate without being told and
sat waiting on the couch until his father
came home from work.
"It's pouring outside," said Papa as he
walked in the door.

"Time to put on your costume," said Mama.
   Mickey turned as white as a ghost. Jenna gasped.
   Mama looked puzzled, and Papa shook out his
   jacket.
"I left it in the backyard," whispered Mickey.
"We left it in the backyard," whispered Jenna.

Papa retrieved it since he was wet already, but the costume was wetter. The yellow beak was squished and the wings were sopping wet. The feathers fell off one by one.

Mickey started to cry.

"I can't be in the play," he sobbed.

"We'll make you another costume," said Jenna,
running to fetch her box of art supplies.

"Do we have any feathers?" called Papa.

"We don't have any poster board," said Jenna,
returning, "but we have colored markers and
a cardboard box and this old feather duster."

So Mama started cutting and Jenna started drawing and Papa pulled feathers out of the old feather duster. They made Mickey a beak and some wings full of feathers, and they dressed him in his new costume.

"No way," said Mickey.
"I don't look like the others!"
"You're a duck," said Papa.
"You're a blue–and–brown duck,"
  said Jenna.
"The female duck is usually
  brown," said Mama, which
  was a big mistake because
  Mickey didn't want to be
  a female duck at all.
"No way," Mickey said
  once more, and he took
  off his costume.

Jenna had an idea. She took Mickey into the bedroom and pulled a book off the shelf.

"There are all different kinds of ducks," said Jenna.
"We'll find one that looks like you. How about the
 mallard?"
"My head's not green," said Mickey.

"How about the
cinnamon teal?"
said Jenna. "He's
nice and brown."
"I don't like the taste of cinnamon,"
said Mickey.
"What about the pintail?" said Jenna.
"It sounds like a party game," said Mickey,
but his face brightened as he pointed to
a picture. "I'll be him," he said.

I am a blue-winged teal from Saskatchewan, Ontario, Kansas, Missouri, Illinois, Ohio, and New Jersey

And the show went on.
Mickey was happy as he quacked like a duck and sang
his duck song and flapped his brown-and-blue wings, with
a sign across his chest that said, "I am a blue-winged teal
from Saskatchewan, Ontario, Kansas, Missouri, Illinois, Ohio,
and New Jersey."

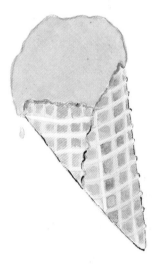

By the time the play was over,
the rain had stopped. Mama,
Papa, and Jenna took Mickey
out for ice cream.
Mickey chose pistachio.
"Ducks like green," he said.
Papa chose peach, and Mama
chose low-fat vanilla.
Jenna chose chocolate, because
she always did.

"Four different flavors!" Jenna announced.

"Like in my play!" said Mickey.

And they all happily ate their different ice creams.